SCHOLASTIC

Charts, Tables & Graphs

30 Skill-Building Reproducible Pages
That Prepare Kids for Standardized Tests

by
Michael Priestley

New York • Toronto • London • Auckland • Sydney
Mexico City • New Delhi • Hong Kong • Buenos Aires

Teaching *Resources*

Scholastic Inc. grants teachers permission to photocopy the designated reproducible pages from this book for classroom use. No other part of this publication may be reproduced in whole or in part, or stored in a retrieval system, or transmitted in any form or by any means, electronic, mechanical, photocopying, recording, or otherwise, without written permission of the publisher. For information regarding permission, write to Scholastic Inc., 557 Broadway, New York, NY 10012.

Cover design by Maria Lilja
Interior design by Creative Pages, Inc.
Interior illustrations by Mark Mason

ISBN 0-439-51775-3

Contents

Contents *(continued)*

INTRODUCTION

Welcome to *FunnyBone Books*: *Charts, Tables & Graphs*. This book provides you with a fun way to:

- help students learn how to read charts and tables;
- marvel at the mysteries of pictographs;
- stop time with a time line;
- open students' eyes to the wonders of stem-and-leaf diagrams; and
- travel to distant lands via scatterplot.

Along the way, you and your students will learn lots of fascinating things, and you'll soon be able to answer some tough questions that everyone should know, such as:

How long did Vernon Kruger of South Africa sit inside a barrel?
Does fast food make you smarter?
How many kids at Spicoli High School colored their hair in 2004?
When was frozen food invented?
Do armadillos really sleep 19 hours a day?

In the everyday world students cope with scads of information, some in the form of visual displays: tables, graphs, scatterplots, and so on. Students need to know how to read these displays to get the straight facts. Statistics and other kinds of data can be used to present information clearly and concisely. They can also be used to distort and misrepresent information. (For some reason, advertising and politics just happen to come to mind!) Students need to be able to tell the difference between an honest graph and a devious one. They also need to know how to construct charts, graphs, and tables. We'll touch on that subject occasionally in this book, too, but mostly that's a story for another time and place. . . .

This book provides 38 activities involving charts, tables, and graphs with a fairly wide range of complexity. Younger students and those who are less familiar with graphic displays might want to spend more time on the first part of this book—especially the first ten activities. These one-page activities provide detailed explanations of how to read and interpret each of ten different kinds of displays. They also provide lots of tips to help students understand exactly what they're looking at.

The next few pages after that—activities 11 and 12—impart great and wonderful wisdom about how to construct graphs from data and how to tell when graphs are trying to mislead you.

In the rest of the book, students may caper and frolic through one- and two-page activities involving bar graphs and circle graphs, line plots and time lines. They will find two or more examples of each kind of display they encountered in the first part of the book—only these examples are a little bigger, a little tougher, and a little more challenging.

So, get these pages into your students' hands without delay, and let the enlightenment begin!

1 Chart: That's a Long Time!

How long could you sit in a barrel? How long do you think you could live in a tree? People have set many time records doing all kinds of wacky things. Take a look at this chart to learn about a few unusual records. Then answer the questions.

Longest Time Spent Doing Stuff

Activity	Name of Person(s)	Time Spent
Standing in a tub of ice cubes	Wim Hof (Netherlands)	1 hr 6 min
Beating on a drum	Paskaran Srcekaram (Singapore)	27 hr 45 min
Kissing on television	Rick Langley and Louisa Almedovar (USA)	30 hr 59 min
Watching movies	Chinnawatra Boomrasn, et al. (Thailand)	50 hr 55 min
Lying on a bed of nails	Inge Wilda Svinjen (Norway)	274 hours
Sitting in a barrel	Vernon Kruger (South Africa)	67 days
Staying in a tree	Bungkas (Indonesia)	21 years

Source: *Guinness Book of Records,* 2004

1. What is the longest time spent sitting in a barrel? _____

2. Who holds the record for the longest time spent standing in a tub of ice cubes? _____

3. What is the record for longest time kissing on TV? _____

4. What is the record for the longest time spent watching movies? _____

5. Who holds the record for the longest time spent lying on a bed of nails? _____

Charts, Tables & Graphs

Scholastic Teaching Resources

Name _____ Date _____

2 Table: Cold Enough for Ya?

Every New Year's Day, members of the Jacksonport Polar Bear Club gather at the shore of Lake Michigan, strip down to their bathing suits, and plunge into the icy water! Look at the table for details on this zany event. Then answer the questions.

Polar Bear Plunges (1993–2004)

Year	Number of Participants	Air Temperature (Fahrenheit)
1993	23	4°
1994	52	33°
1995	71	18°
1996	106	22°
1997	110	25°
1998	290	34°
1999	175	10°
2000	600	33°
2001	700	26°
2002	700	30°
2003	800	28°
2004	600	32°

Source: Jacksonport Polar Bear Club (www.doorbell.net/pbc)

1. In which two years did the Polar Bears have the coldest air temperatures for their plunge?

   _____

2. In what year did the greatest number of people take part in this event, and in what year did the fewest take the plunge?

   _____

3. In general, how has the popularity of this event changed over the years since 1993? Tell how you know.

   _____

4. What do you notice about the changes in the number of participants and the air temperatures from 1998 to 1999? Do you think these two factors are related?

   _____

Read each question carefully to make sure you understand what information it's asking for.

Name _____   Date _____

3 Circle Graph: And If You Believe THAT One . . .

Ms. Hearditall keeps track of hard-to-believe excuses her students give for
not doing their homework. Check out this circle graph to find out what
kinds of excuses Ms. Hearditall gets. Then answer the questions.

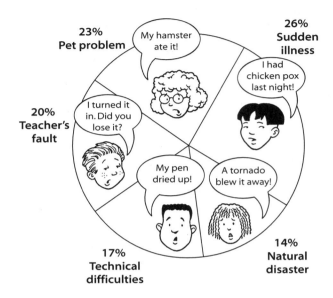

1. Which kind of excuse do Ms. Hearditall's students give most often?

   _____

2. What percentage of the excuses are "pet problems"?   _____

3. Find the percentage of "teacher's fault" excuses.
   How is this number written as a fraction?   _____

4. Which kind of excuse makes up 17% of the total?

   _____

5. Which kind of excuse is used *least*?

   _____

TIP Circle graphs are sometimes called "pie charts" because they
sort of look like pies sliced in different ways. Each "slice"
represents a portion or percentage of the total pie. All the
pieces added together should equal 100 percent.

Charts, Tables & Graphs

Scholastic Teaching Resources

4 Pictograph: Better Skip the Dessert

In 2003, Sonya Thomas set a stomach-popping world record by eating 65 boiled eggs in 6 minutes and 40 seconds! To burn off that 5,000-calorie meal, Sonya probably needed to do a little exercise. Look at the pictograph to find out just how much exercise time that would take. Then answer the questions.

Exercise Time Needed to Burn 5,000 Calories

Bicycling	🕐🕐🕐🕐🕐🕐🕐🕐🕐🕐🕐🕐🕐
In-line skating	🕐🕐🕐🕐🕐🕐🕐🕐🕐🕐🕐🕐🕐🕐
Jumping rope	🕐🕐🕐🕐🕐🕐🕐🕐🕐🕐
Running	🕐🕐🕐🕐🕐🕐🕐🕐
Swimming	🕐🕐🕐🕐🕐🕐🕐🕐
Step aerobics	🕐🕐🕐🕐🕐🕐🕐🕐🕐🕐

KEY: 🕐 = 1 hour of exercise

Source: International Federation of Competitive Eating and fitresource.com

1. Which exercise burns calories the fastest? _____

2. Which exercise would Sonya have to do for the longest time to burn off 5,000 calories? _____

3. Which two exercises burn calories at the same rate? _____

4. To burn off 5,000 calories, how long would Sonya have to swim? _____

5. Which exercise takes about 13 hours to burn 5,000 calories? _____

TIP
To read a pictograph, look for the key that tells what each picture represents.

Name _____ Date _____

5 Bar Graph: The Need for Speed

Did you ever wonder where you can find the fastest roller coasters in the world, or how fast they really go? Well, here's your chance to find out. Check out this bar graph. Then answer the questions.

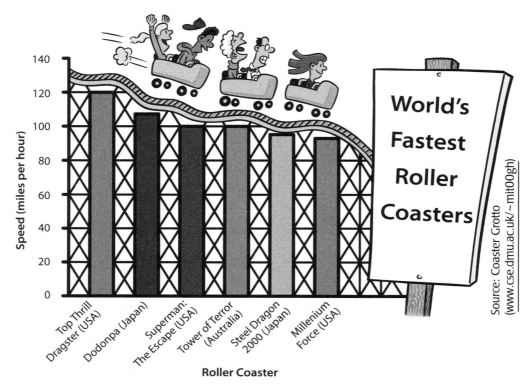

Source: Coaster Grotto (www.cse.dmu.ac.uk/~mit00gh)

1. Which is the fastest roller coaster? _____

2. How fast does the fastest roller coaster go? _____

3. Which two roller coasters have the same top speed?

_____

4. What is the name of the fastest coaster outside the United States?

_____

5. What is the top speed for Steel Dragon 2000? _____

Bar graphs are good for making comparisons—just compare the lengths of the bars.

Charts, Tables & Graphs

Scholastic Teaching Resources

6 Line Graph: A Gassy Subject

Have you ever heard an old-timer say, "Gee, when I was a kid, you could get a gallon of gas for a quarter"? Well, that was probably true. But look at this graph to see what gasoline costs now! Then answer the questions.

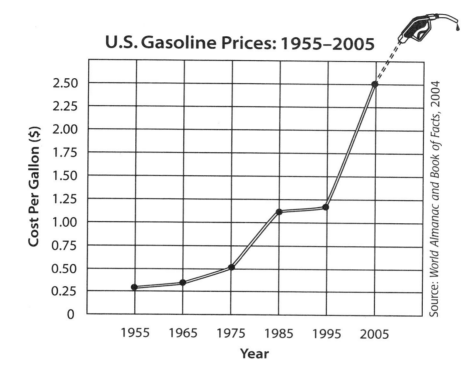

U.S. Gasoline Prices: 1955–2005

Source: World Almanac and Book of Facts, 2004

1. How much did a gallon of gasoline cost in 1955? _____

2. When you look at the graph, what do you notice about 1985 and 1995?

   _____

3. Which 10-year period saw the greatest increase in the price of gasoline? _____

4. How much has the price of gasoline changed since 1955? _____

TIP

A line graph is used to show a change that occurs over a certain period of time. Sometimes a dotted line is used to estimate or predict what will happen next.

Charts, Tables & Graphs

Name _____   Date _____

7 Line Plot: Who Needs the Elevator?

The Empire State Building Run-Up may just be the world's wackiest race.
Each year, racers of all ages scramble up 1,576 steps to the Observatory
deck on the 86th floor of the famous New York skyscraper. Look at the
line plot to see how quickly the nimblest racers reach the top. Then answer
the questions.

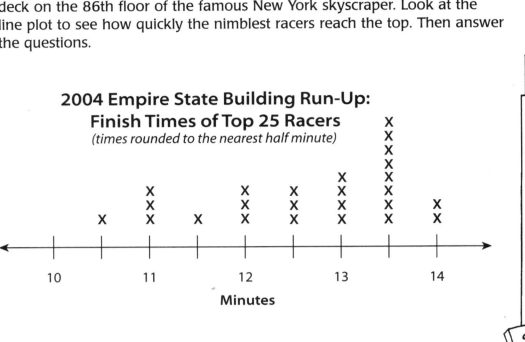

2004 Empire State Building Run-Up:
Finish Times of Top 25 Racers
(times rounded to the nearest half minute)

Minutes

Source: Empire State Building (www.esbnyc.com)

1. What was the winner's time for the race?   _____

2. How many racers finished in 13 minutes or less?   _____

3. What was the most common finish time among
   the top 25 racers?   _____

4. How many racers finished in less than 12 minutes?   _____

5. What general trend (or shape) do you see in these data?

_____

> A line plot can be used to show the "shape" of a set of results,
> or data. It kind of resembles a tally chart, only it faces upward
> instead of sideways. Each X is one result, or data point. Results
> often bunch up in the middle or at one end of the line.

Charts, Tables & Graphs

Scholastic Teaching Resources

8 Time Line: Oldies but Goodies

The world's best toys have never gone out of style. Some all-time favorites have been around since your great-grandparents were in diapers. Use this time line to find out when some classic toys were invented. Then answer the questions.

20th-Century Toys

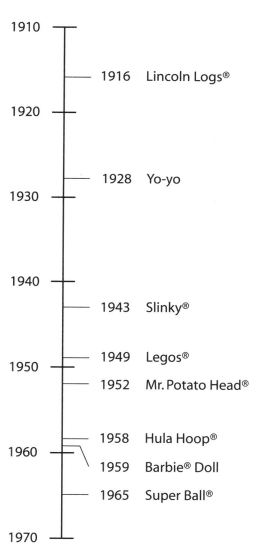

1910	
1916	Lincoln Logs®
1920	
1928	Yo-yo
1930	
1940	
1943	Slinky®
1949	Legos®
1950	
1952	Mr. Potato Head®
1958	Hula Hoop®
1960	
1959	Barbie® Doll
1965	Super Ball®
1970	

Source: Great Idea Finder (www.ideafinder.com)

1. What is the oldest toy shown on the time line?

   _____

2. In what year did Barbie® dolls first appear?

   _____

3. Which two toys were introduced in the 1940s?

   _____

   _____

4. When was Mr. Potato Head® introduced?

   _____

5. What toy appeared 30 years after the yo-yo was introduced?

   _____

> **TIP**
>
> Time lines usually show important events—when they happened and in what sequence. Time lines may be vertical (like this one), horizontal, or diagonal.

Scholastic Teaching Resources

Charts, Tables & Graphs

Name _____ Date _____

9 Stem-and-Leaf Diagram: Football Follies

Between 1979 and 1982, the Wildcats football team of Northwestern University racked up a 34-game losing streak—a record in college football. When the team lost, they often lost in a big way! Look at the stem-and-leaf diagram to see how many points the Wildcats lost by in each game. Then answer the questions.

Number of Points Wildcats Lost Games by During 34-Game Losing Streak

Stem	Leaf
0	1 4 7 9
1	2 4 5 6
2	0 1 1 2 5 6 8
3	0 0 0 1 2 3 5 5 6 7 8 8
4	2 7
5	2 2
6	3 4 4

Source: College Football Data Warehouse (www.cfbdatawarehouse.com)

1. What is the smallest number of points the Wildcats ever lost by during the streak? _____

2. What is the greatest number of points the Wildcats ever lost by during the streak? _____

3. How many games did the Wildcats lose by more than 40 points? _____

4. How many games did the Wildcats lose by fewer than 20 points? _____

5. How many times did the Wildcats lose by exactly 30 points? _____

A stem-and-leaf diagram is a kind of graph used to display a set of data. In this kind of diagram, a "leaf" is the "ones" digit in a number, and the "stem" is the rest of the number (to the left of the "ones" digit). For example:

Stem	Leaf		Number
0	4	=	4
3	5	=	35
19	2	=	192

14   Charts, Tables & Graphs

Scholastic Teaching Resources

10 Scatterplot: Giant Pumpkins

Have you ever seen a really, *really* big pumpkin? Chances are, it was a midget next to these babies—the biggest pumpkins ever grown in the United States and Canada. Use the scatterplot at right to find the weights of the heftiest pumpkins grown in recent years. Then answer the questions.

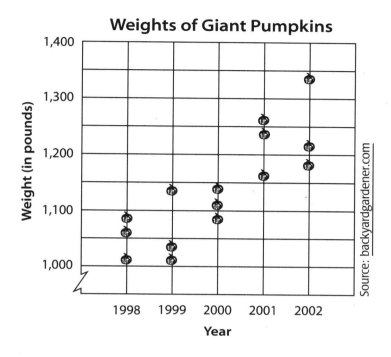

Weights of Giant Pumpkins

Source: backyardgardener.com

1. About how much did the heaviest giant pumpkin weigh?

   _____

2. In what year did all three giant pumpkins weigh less than 1,100 pounds?

   _____

3. In which two years did the heaviest pumpkin weigh between 1,125 and 1,150 pounds?

   _____

4. What trend do you notice in these data? Describe the trend and tell whether it is positive or negative.

   _____

   _____

A scatterplot shows data points based on **two** values—such as height and weight, for example. The data points on a scatterplot may show a positive trend, which means that as one value goes up, the other value does, too. For example, as you grow taller, your weight increases. The scatterplot may show a negative trend instead, or no trend at all.

Charts, Tables & Graphs

Name _____ Date _____

11 Constructing Graphs

Let's try making some charts and graphs! Each kind of display can be used to present certain kinds of information. For each exercise below, read the information given. Choose the best kind of display to present the information and construct your display. Be sure to label your displays clearly and correctly.

Exercise 1: Teens' Time

Claudia took a survey to see what teenagers do in their spare time. Here are the results of the survey. Construct a graph to show these results.

Activity	Amount of Time Spent
Playing sports	25%
Listening to music	10%
Playing video games	15%
Talking on phone	10%
Chilling	25%
Watching TV	15%

Exercise 2: Bug Bites

Timothy made a tally chart to keep track of how many bug bites he got during a camping trip. Make a display to show these results.

Day	Bug Bites
1	✓ ✓ ✓ ✓ ✓ ✓
2	✓ ✓ ✓ ✓
3	✓ ✓ ✓ ✓ ✓ ✓ ✓
4	✓ ✓ ✓ ✓ ✓
5	✓ ✓ ✓ ✓ ✓ ✓ ✓ ✓

Scholastic Teaching Resources

Charts, Tables & Graphs

Name _____   Date _____

Constructing Graphs (continued)

Exercise 3: Exotic Pet Sales

Margo's Pet Store sells exotic and unusual pets. The chart below shows how many pets Margo sold last month. Make a display to present these data.

Type of Pet	Number Sold
Lizards	12
Ferrets	6
Snails	5
Fighting fish	8
Snakes	9
Talking birds	11

Exercise 4: Friendship Bracelets

Tori and Megan started making and selling friendship bracelets at the beginning of the summer. Before long, sales were booming! Make a display to show their sales record for the first six weeks.

Week	Sales
1	$25
2	$30
3	$45
4	$80
5	$75
6	$90

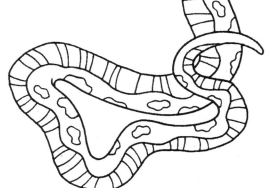

Name _____ Date _____

12 Representing Data

Sometimes graphs can be used to make data look or sound better by presenting information in misleading ways. For example, advertisements might present information in ways that make consumer products more appealing. In politics, information can be used in positive or negative ways to make a candidate look better or worse.

In the exercises below, look at each graph closely to see if it might be misleading. Then answer the questions that follow.

1. The circle graph below shows the results of a voters' poll. Voters were asked which candidate they planned to vote for in the next election.

Percentage of Voters Who Plan to Vote for Each Candidate

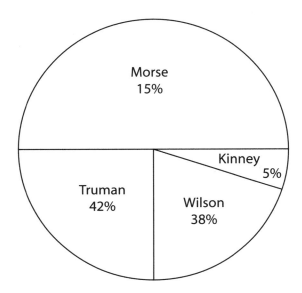

a. According to this graph, which candidates are leading the race?

_____

b. How is this graph misleading? _____

_____

Charts, Tables & Graphs

Name _____ Date _____

Representing Data *(continued)*

2. These two graphs compare the sales and prices of two brands of ice cream. Think about what these graphs show. Then answer the questions.

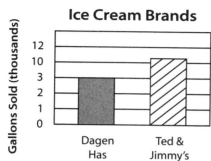

a. What does the "Ice Cream Brands" graph suggest about Dagen Has ice cream, and how is the graph misleading?

_____

_____

b. What does the "Ice Cream Prices" graph suggest about Ted & Jimmy's ice cream, and how is the graph misleading?

_____

_____

3. These line graphs show changes in the costs of movie tickets and movie rentals from 2001 to 2004. Take a look at the graphs. Then answer the questions.

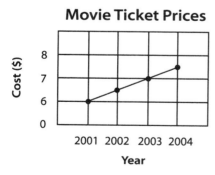

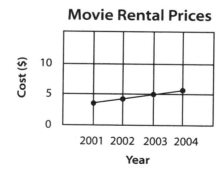

a. According to these graphs, how did the costs of movie tickets and movie rentals change from 2001 to 2004?

_____

b. How are these graphs misleading?

_____

_____

13 Charts: Hollywood Winners and Losers

A movie makes money when ticket sales add up to more than the cost of making the movie. Big Hollywood hits rake in millions of dollars, but big duds *lose* millions. Take a gander at these charts to see the biggest winners and biggest losers in Hollywood. Then answer the questions.

Big Money-Making Movies in U.S. Theaters (2003)

Title	Ticket Sales (millions)	Cost to Make (millions)	Net Earnings (millions)
Titanic	$600.8	$200	$400.8
Star Wars	$461	$11	$450
E.T.—the Extra-Terrestrial	$434.9	$10.5	$424.4
Star Wars: Episode 1—The Phantom Menace	$431.1	$115	$316.1
Spider-Man	$403.7	$139	$264.7
Lord of the Rings: The Return of the King	$377	$94	$283
Jurassic Park	$357.1	$63	$294.1
Lord of the Rings: The Two Towers	$341.7	$94	$247.7
Finding Nemo	$339.7	$94	$245.7
Forrest Gump	$329.7	$55	$274.7

Big Money-Losing Movies in U.S. Theaters (2003)

Title	Ticket Sales (millions)	Cost to Make (millions)	Net Loss (millions)
Heaven's Gate	$1.5	$44	$42.5
The Adventures of Pluto Nash	$4.4	$100	$95.6
Monkeybone	$5.4	$75	$69.6
Town & Country	$6.7	$90	$83.3
Cutthroat Island	$11	$92	$81
3000 Miles to Graceland	$15.7	$62	$46.3
Hudson Hawk	$17	$65	$48
Battlefield Earth	$21.5	$73	$51.5
The Postman	$27	$80	$53
Treasure Planet	$37	$140	$103

Source: worldwideboxoffice.com

When you are looking at two similar charts, make sure you look at the right one to find the information you need.

Scholastic Teaching Resources

Hollywood Winners and Losers *(continued)*

1. Which three money-making movies cost the most to make?

    _____

    _____

    _____

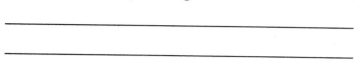

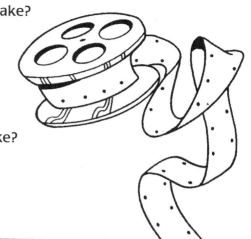

2. Which two money-making movies cost the least to make?

    _____

    _____

3. How much did *Titanic* collect in U.S. ticket sales? _____

4. Which movie ranks first in the total amount of net earnings?

    _____

5. How much more did *Finding Nemo* make in ticket sales than *Forrest Gump*?

    _____

6. Which two money-losing movies had the greatest net losses?

    _____

    _____

7. Of the ten money-losing movies listed, how many cost more than $40 million to make? _____

8. Which money-losing movie had the lowest ticket sales?

    _____

9. How much did *Monkeybone* cost to make?

    _____

10. How much more did *The Postman* make in ticket sales than *Hudson Hawk*?

    _____

14 Charts: Daredevils of Niagara Falls

Most people feel a thrill just by gazing at Niagara Falls from a safe distance. But Niagara Falls has attracted more than its share of daredevils. Some have plummeted over the edge of the falls, while others have crossed over on tightropes. Read the charts to learn about some of these thrill-seekers. Then answer the questions.

Stunt Rides Over Niagara Falls

Name of Person(s)	Year	Type of Vessel
Annie Taylor	1901	wooden barrel
Bobby Leach	1911	steel barrel
Jean Lussier	1928	rubber ball with steel frame
Nathan Boya	1961	rubber ball with steel frame (exact copy of Lussier's craft)
Karl Soucek	1984	metal and fiberglass barrel
Steven Trotter	1985	plastic barrel wrapped with rubber tubes
David Munday	1985	steel barrel
Peter Debernardi and Jeffrey Petkovich	1989	steel barrel
David Munday	1995	steel barrel
Steven Trotter and Lori Martin	1995	steel barrel coated with Kevlar®

Tightrope Crossings Over Niagara Falls

Name of Person(s)	Year	Special Feat(s)
Jean François Gravelet	1859	first person to cross Niagara Falls on tightrope; did a somersault and drank from a bottle on rope
William Leonard Hunt	1860	crossed with an old-fashioned washing machine strapped on his back
Andrew Jenkins	1869	rode across tightrope on a bicycle
Maria Spelterina	1876	first woman to cross Niagara Falls on a tightrope; walked backwards, wore a paper bag on her head, and walked with baskets attached to her feet
Clifford Calverley	1892	set a speed record by making a crossing in 6 minutes and 32.5 seconds

Source: niagaraparks.com

Charts, Tables & Graphs

Daredevils of Niagara Falls *(continued)*

1. Which stunt rider went over Niagara Falls in a wooden barrel?

   _____

2. Who was the first person to cross Niagara Falls on a tightrope?

   _____

3. In what year did Maria Spelterina cross Niagara Falls on a tightrope?

   _____

4. What type of vessel did Steven Trotter use for his first ride over Niagara Falls?

   _____

5. How were the stunt rides of Jean Lussier and Nathan Boya alike?

   _____

6. What pairs of stunt riders rode over Niagara Falls together?

   _____

7. What special feat did William Leonard Hunt do on a tightrope over Niagara Falls?

   _____

8. In what years did David Munday ride over Niagara Falls in a barrel?

   _____

9. How long did it take Clifford Calverley to cross Niagara Falls on a tightrope?

   _____

10. Who made a tightrope crossing on a bicycle?

   _____

Name _____ Date _____

15 Table: Wacky Weight Watchers

Many people know that it's much easier to jump on the moon because it has lower gravity than Earth, so you weigh less. But have you ever wondered what would happen if you could travel to the other planets in the solar system? A planet's size determines how heavy an object on its surface will be. Check out the table below to see how heavy different objects would be on different planets. Then answer the questions.

Weights of Objects Across the Solar System (in pounds)

Planet	Object				
	Baseball Bat	Watermelon	Standard Poodle	Sofa	Hippopotamus
Earth	2.5	12	55	225	8,000
Mercury	0.9	4.5	20.7	85	3,024
Venus	2.2	10.8	49.8	204	7,256
Mars	0.9	4.5	20.7	84.8	3,016
Jupiter	5.9	28.3	130	531.9	18,912
Saturn	2.6	12.7	58.5	239.4	8,512
Uranus	2.2	10.6	48.8	200	7,112
Neptune	2.8	13.5	61.8	253.1	9,000
Pluto	0.1	0.8	3.6	15	536

Source: *World Almanac and Book of Facts*, 2004

Charts, Tables & Graphs

Wacky Weight Watchers *(continued)*

1. On which planet are watermelons and sofas heaviest? _____

2. On which planet are poodles and hippos lightest? _____

3. How much does a baseball bat weigh on Venus? _____
   On Neptune? _____

4. On which planet does a standard poodle weigh about 130 pounds?

   _____

5. On which planet do things weigh the closest to what they weigh on Earth?

   _____

6. On which two planets does a watermelon weigh exactly the same amount?

   _____   _____

7. How much less does a sofa weigh on Pluto than on Earth? _____

8. How much does a hippopotamus weigh on Mercury? _____
   On Uranus? _____

9. Are things heavier on Venus or on Neptune? _____

10. What is your weight on Earth? Using the information
    in the table, estimate how much you would weigh on Mars. _____

Name _____ Date _____

16 Tables: Feeling Sheepish

Are there more people or more animals where you live? If you live
in a city this might be hard to imagine, but in some places the livestock
far outnumber the people. Imagine if your town had more than 300
sheep per person, for example, as in the Falkland Islands. That's a lot
of sheep's wool for sweaters! Look at the tables below to answer the
questions on the next page.

Table 1: Ten Countries Where Sheep Outnumber People (2000)

Country	Number of Sheep	Human Population	Sheep per Person
Falkland Islands (part of the U.K.)	717,000	2,121	338.05
New Zealand	47,144,000	3,494,300	13.49
Uruguay	22,685,000	3,116,800	7.28
Australia	120,651,000	18,114,000	6.66
Mongolia	13,719,000	2,363,000	5.81
Mauritania	5,288,000	2,217,000	2.39
Kazakhstan	33,524,000	16,963,600	1.98
Iceland	470,000	266,800	1.76
Namibia	2,620,000	1,500,000	1.75
Somalia	13,500,000	9,077,000	1.45

Source: *The Top 10 of Everything: 1998* (DK Publishing)

Now, what about in the United States? Do sheep outnumber people?
No, but the numbers of sheep and numbers of people have changed
considerably over the last 100 years or so—as you can see in the
table below.

Table 2: U.S. Populations of Sheep and Humans (1900–2000)

Year	Number of Sheep (in millions)	Number of People (in millions)
1900	48.1	76.2
1920	40.7	106.0
1940	52.1	132.2
1960	33.2	179.3
1980	12.7	226.5
2000	7.0	281.4

Source: *World Almanac and Book of Facts*, 2004

Scholastic Teaching Resources

Charts, Tables & Graphs

Feeling Sheepish *(continued)*

1. Which country in Table 1 has the largest number of sheep?

   _____

2. Which country in Table 1 has the smallest human population?

   _____

3. How many sheep are there per person in Mongolia? _____

4. How many countries listed in Table 1
   have more than 10 million sheep? _____

5. Which countries have more than 10 sheep per person?

   _____

6. According to Table 2, how many sheep
   were there in the United States in 1900? _____

7. In 1920, how did the population of sheep compare with the number of people
   in the United States?

   _____

8. What was the U.S. population (of humans) in 1940? _____

9. What has happened to the sheep and human populations in the United States
   since 1900?

   _____

10. In 2000, which countries listed in Table 1 had more sheep than the United States?

    _____

    _____

Name _____ Date _____

17 Circle Graphs: A Pretty Penny

What would you say if someone asked you what kind of metal a penny was made of? Copper? Well, you'd be right . . . if you were living before 1837! Actually, pennies still contained a fair amount of copper until recently, but the copper was mixed with other metals. The composition of the penny has changed many times, and now copper is only used to coat the outside of the coin! Find out how the penny has changed by looking at the graphs below. Then answer the questions.

The Changing Composition of a Penny

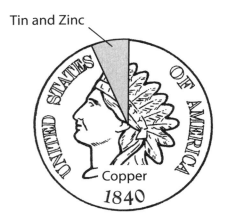

1837–1857 and 1864–1962

1857–1864

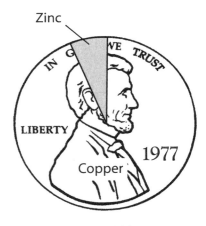

1962–1982

1982–present

Source: usmint.gov

In a circle graph, the entire circle represents 100 percent. Each portion of the circle represents some part of that, based on the size of the portion. For example, one-half of the circle represents 50 percent.

Charts, Tables & Graphs

Name _____ Date _____ **29**

A Pretty Penny *(continued)*

1. During what time period did the penny contain the least amount of copper?

   _____

2. From 1857 to 1864, about what percentage of a penny was nickel?

   _____

3. During which time periods did the penny contain the same percentage of copper?

   _____

4. Approximately how much copper does a penny contain now? _____

5. **Make your own graph.** Suppose that the composition of a penny changed to 20% aluminum, 40% zinc, and 40% copper. Make a circle graph to show these figures.

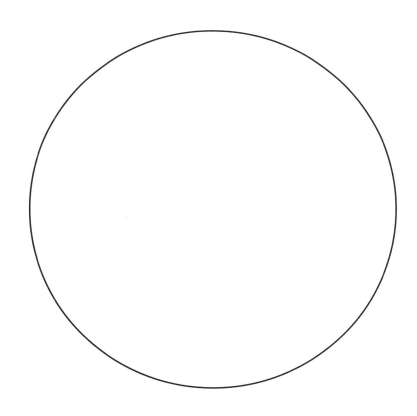

Name _____ Date _____

18 Circle Graphs: Sawing Wood

Have you ever been kept awake all night because someone was snoring—which is sometimes called "sawing wood"? Or maybe *you* are the one who snores and keep other people awake! Don't worry, though, because many people snore. Compare the graphs below to see how snoring is different for kids and adults. Then answer the questions.

Percentage of Adults Who Snore

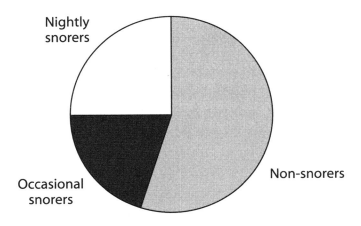

Percentage of Kids Who Snore

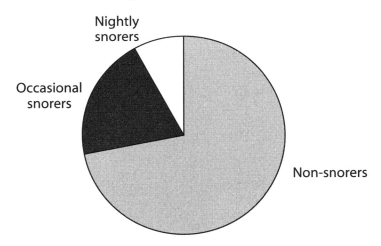

Source: Scientific American (www.sciam.com)

Charts, Tables & Graphs

Scholastic Teaching Resources

Sawing Wood *(continued)*

1. Do more adults or more kids snore nightly?

   _____

2. About what percentage of adults are nightly snorers?

   _____

3. Are there more adults who are nightly snorers or more who are occasional snorers?

   _____

4. Approximately what percentage of kids snore sometimes or all the time? _____

5. In a group of 1,000 kids, approximately how many of them generally do not snore? _____

6. If you combined the information from both of these graphs in a new graph for people of all ages, what would it look like? Complete the new graph below. Remember to label each part.

Percentage of People Who Snore

19 Pictograph: TV Nations

Did you know that there are 844 TV sets for every 1,000 people in the United States? Many countries have considerably fewer TVs than we do. For example, the pictograph below shows the number of TVs in several countries.

TV Sets in Different Countries (per 1,000 people)

Country	Number of TV Sets
Algeria	📺📺📺📺📺📺📺📺📺📺🭬
Cameroon	📺📺📺🭬
Ethiopia	🭬
Iraq	📺📺📺📺📺📺📺🭬
Mali	📺🭬
Nigeria	📺📺📺📺📺📺
Syria	📺📺📺📺📺🭬
Uganda	📺📺🭬
Zambia	📺📺📺📺📺📺📺📺📺📺📺📺📺🭬
Zimbabwe	📺📺📺🭬

Source: *World Almanac and Book of Facts*, 2004

Key: 📺 = 10 TV sets

1. How many TV sets does Algeria have (per 1,000 people)? _____

2. Which country has the fewest TV sets (per 1,000 people)? _____

3. Which countries have more than 100 TV sets (per 1,000 people)?

   _____

4. How many TV sets are there in Zimbabwe (per 1,000 people)? _____

5. List two countries that have about the same number of TV sets (per 1,000 people).

   _____

Charts, Tables & Graphs

20 Pictograph: Screaming for Ice Cream

How much ice cream do you think you eat in a year? Check out the pictograph below to see if you match up to the average for any of the top ice cream–consuming countries in the world. Then answer the questions.

The World's Biggest Ice-Cream Eaters

Country	Average Number of Pints of Ice Cream Eaten per Person per Year
United States	Ice Cream symbols (14)
Finland	Ice Cream symbols (12½)
Denmark	Ice Cream symbols (11)
Australia	Ice Cream symbols (9)
Canada	Ice Cream symbols (7½)
Sweden	Ice Cream symbols (7)
Norway	Ice Cream symbols (6)
Belgium	Ice Cream symbols (5½)
United Kingdom	Ice Cream symbols (4½)
New Zealand	Ice Cream symbols (4½)

Key: ![icon] = 4 pints

Source: *The Top 10 of Everything: 1998* (DK Publishing)

TIP For each country, count the number of symbols and multiply by the value of a symbol (4 pints).

1. On average, about how much ice cream does a person in Australia eat per year? _____

2. Which country consumes more ice cream per person—Norway or Canada? _____

3. In which country do people eat an average of about 25 pints of ice cream per year? _____

4. When compared with ice-cream eaters in the United States, which countries consume less than half the amount of ice cream per person?

   _____

5. In which countries do people eat 35 or more pints of ice cream per person per year?

   _____

Name _____ Date _____

21 Pictograph: On Vacation—Wish You Were Here!

Do you think Americans take a lot of vacation time? Not really. Compared with people of many other countries, Americans are workaholics. Take a look at the pictograph below to see how we compare. Then answer the questions.

Vacations in Different Countries

Country	Average Days of Paid Vacation Per Year
Australia	🚐🚐🚐🚐🚐
Britain	🚐🚐🚐🚐🚐
China	🚐🚐🚐
Germany	🚐🚐🚐🚐🚐🚐
Japan	🚐🚐🚐🚐̸
Netherlands	🚐🚐🚐🚐🚐̸
Spain	🚐🚐🚐🚐🚐🚐
United States	🚐🚐

Key: 🚐 = 5 days

Source: *U.S. News and World Report* (June 28/July 5, 2004)

1. In which two countries do people have the most vacation time?

   _____ _____

2. How many days of vacation do people take in Japan? _____

3. Which country has the least vacation time?

   _____

4. How long is the average vacation in China? _____

5. In which countries do people take an average of 25 vacation days per year?

   _____

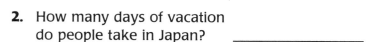

Charts, Tables & Graphs

Name _____ Date _____

22 Bar Graph: Crazy Collections

Have you ever thought about collecting something odd—such as chamber pots or bags of potato chips or refrigerator magnets? People collect all these things and many more. Take a look at this bar graph of odd stuff. Then answer the questions.

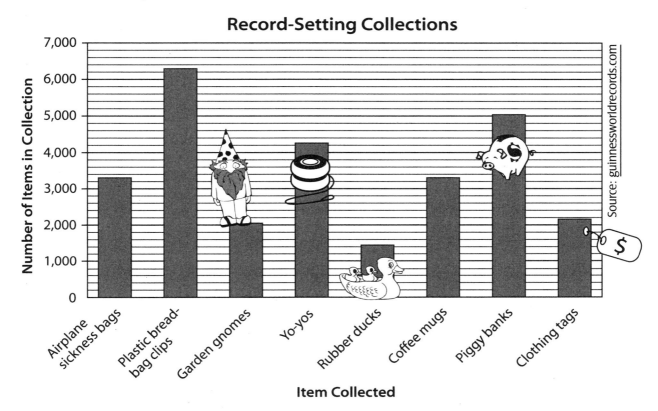

Record-Setting Collections

Number of Items in Collection

Item Collected

Source: guinnessworldrecords.com

1. Which collection has the greatest number of items? _____

2. How many rubber ducks are in the world's largest rubber-duck collection? _____

3. Which collection has about the same number of items as the world's largest collection of clothing tags? _____

4. About how many more piggy banks are there than yo-yos in the record-setting collections? _____

5. How many items are there in the "airplane sickness bags" collection? (Let's hope those bags are empty!) _____

Charts, Tables & Graphs

23 Bar Graphs: That's a Whopper!

What's the biggest thing you've ever eaten? Bet it wasn't as big as the record-setting foods in the graphs below! Chew on this information for a bit. Then answer the questions.

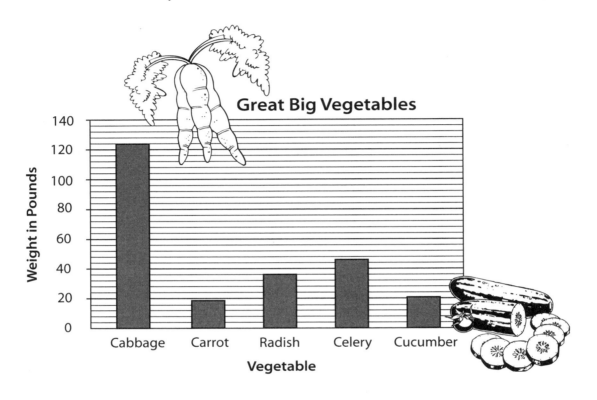

Great Big Vegetables

Weight in Pounds

Cabbage   Carrot   Radish   Celery   Cucumber

Vegetable

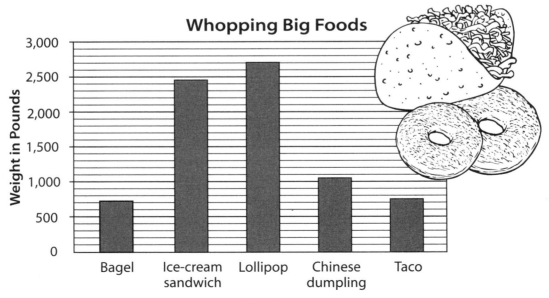

Whopping Big Foods

Weight in Pounds

Bagel   Ice-cream sandwich   Lollipop   Chinese dumpling   Taco

Food

Source: *The Top 10 of Everything: 1998* (DK Publishing)

Charts, Tables & Graphs

That's a Whopper! (continued)

1. Which weighed more—the biggest cabbage or the biggest bagel?

   _____

2. Which record-setting vegetable weighed about 45 pounds?

   _____

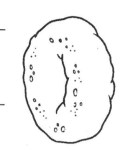

3. How many "Great Big Vegetables" weighed less than the biggest ice-cream sandwich? _____

4. Which record-setting vegetable weighed the least?

   _____

5. About how many pounds did the heaviest lollipop weigh? _____

6. How much heavier is the biggest bagel than the biggest cabbage?

   _____

7. About how much did the world's biggest taco weigh? _____

8. If every person at a coleslaw festival ate one pound of cabbage, how many people would it take to eat the world's biggest cabbage? _____

9. What was the weight of the record-setting Chinese dumpling? _____

10. About how many pounds did the world's biggest ice-cream sandwich weigh? _____

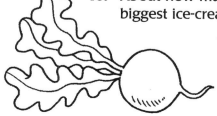
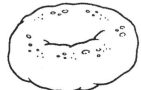

Scholastic Teaching Resources

Charts, Tables & Graphs

Name _____ Date _____

24 Bar Graphs: It's a Wonderful Life!

Did you ever wonder how long animals sleep each day, or how long animals live? Believe you me, there are some pretty lazy animals out there—and some old ones, too. Take a look at the animals in these graphs. Then answer the questions.

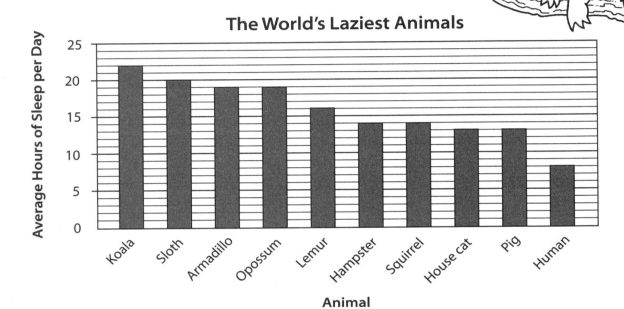

The World's Laziest Animals

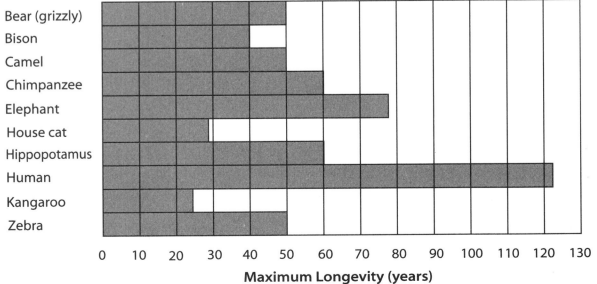

Longest-Living Mammals

Source: *The Top 10 of Everything: 1998* (DK Publishing)

Charts, Tables & Graphs

Scholastic Teaching Resources

Name _____ Date _____

It's a Wonderful Life! *(continued)*

1. Which animals sleep for an average of 14 hours per day?

_____

2. How many of the animals shown on the graph sleep for more than 15 hours per day? _____

3. What was the longest life ever recorded for a camel? _____

4. How old did the oldest elephant live to be? _____

5. On average, how many hours a day does a house cat sleep? _____

6. What was the longest life ever recorded for a house cat? _____

7. Which animal sleeps for an average of 16 hours a day?

_____

8. Which animal sleeps longest of all?

_____

9. Which kind of mammal lived longest of all?

_____

10. How old did the oldest kangaroo live to be? _____

Name _____   Date _____

25 Line Graph: Colors to Dye For

At Spicoli High School, students' hair colors have been changing in recent years. Dozens of students now have orange, purple, green, or blue hair! Could it be something in the local water supply? Scan the line graph below to see what has been happening. Then answer the questions.

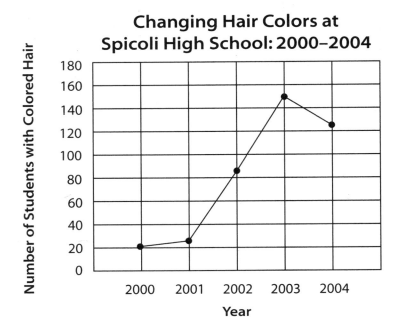

Changing Hair Colors at Spicoli High School: 2000–2004

1. How many students at Spicoli High School had colored hair in 2000? _____

2. In 2002, how many students colored their hair? _____

3. Can you tell from this graph how many students had purple hair in 2001? Explain.

   _____

4. What happened to the number of students with colored hair from 2003 to 2004?

   _____

5. Based on the information in this graph, how many students do you think will have colored hair in 2005? _____

Name _____   Date _____

26 Line Graph: Frog Heaven

There is a pond in Tino's neighborhood, and he likes to go there to catch frogs. Last year he conducted an experiment to see how the frog population changes each month. Look at the line graph below to see the results of his study. Then answer the questions.

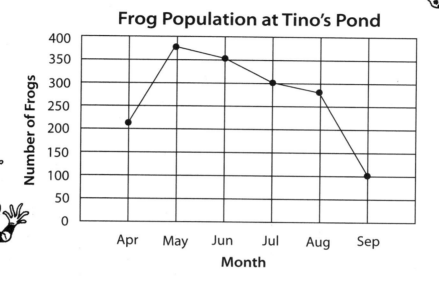

Frog Population at Tino's Pond

1. How many frogs were there in Tino's pond in April? _____

2. What happened to the frog population from April to May?

    _____

3. How many frogs were there in July? _____

4. In which two months did the frog population stay almost the same?

    _____   _____

5. Based on the information in this graph, estimate the frog population at Tino's pond in October. _____

Scholastic Teaching Resources

27 Line Graphs: Hello? Are You There?

Does it sometimes seem that everywhere you look, people are talking on cell phones or instant messaging friends on the Internet? Well, they are— and in huge numbers! Look at the line graphs below to see just how many people are on the grid. Then answer the questions.

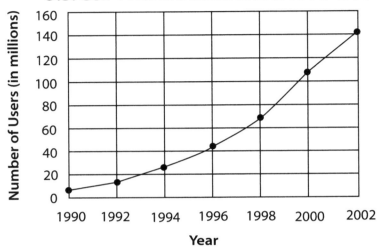

Source: *World Almanac and Book of Facts,* 2004

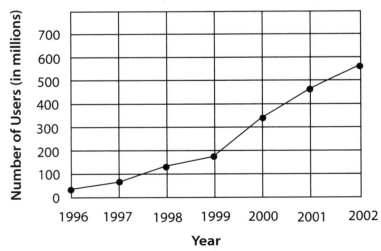

Source: Global Policy Forum (www.globalpolicy.org)

Charts, Tables & Graphs

Scholastic Teaching Resources

Hello? Are You There? *(continued)*

1. About how many Americans used cell phones in 1990? _____

2. In what year did the number of people in the United States using cell phones reach 50 million? _____

3. How many people were using the Internet in 1996? _____

4. How many people were using the Internet in 1998? _____

5. Which one-year period saw the greatest increase in the number of Internet users? _____

6. Describe the rate of increase in cell-phone use from 1990 through 1996.

   _____

7. How many Americans used cell phones in 2002? _____

8. Based on the information shown in the graphs, estimate the number of cell-phone users in the U.S. in 2005. _____

9. Estimate the number of Internet users in 2005. _____

10. What similarity do you notice in these two graphs?

   _____

   _____

28 Line Graph: Fore!

Before Tiger Woods came putting along, it was hard to imagine that anyone could make a lot of money playing golf. But professional golfers today can do very well indeed. Look at the graph below to see how much money the leading players have made over the last 50 years. Then answer the questions.

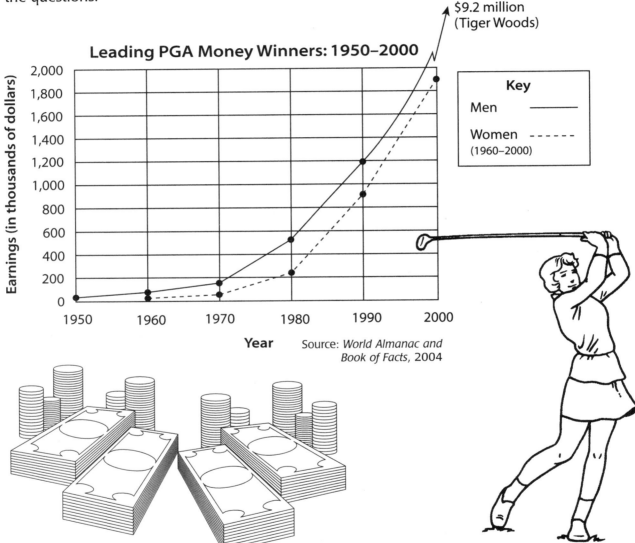

Leading PGA Money Winners: 1950–2000

$9.2 million (Tiger Woods)

Earnings (in thousands of dollars)

Key

Men ————

Women ------
(1960–2000)

Year

Source: *World Almanac and Book of Facts*, 2004

TIP

This display is a double line graph. Use the key to find out what the two different lines represent. Double line graphs are used to compare two similar things as they change—in this case, earnings by men and women golfers. (Note that Tiger Woods's earnings in 2002 were so far off the scale that they did not fit on the graph!)

Fore! *(continued)*

1. About how much did the men's leading
   money winner earn in 1960?   _____

2. About how much did the women's leading
   money winner earn in 1970?   _____

3. How did the men's and women's earnings compare in 1980?

   _____

4. How much did the leading women's earnings
   increase from 1980 to 1990?   _____

5. Based on the data shown in the graph,
   estimate the leading women's earnings
   in 2010.   _____

6. Estimate the change in the leading men's
   earnings from 1960 to 1990.   _____

7. Which year shows the greatest difference
   between men's earnings and women's
   earnings?   _____

8. Describe two trends that you see in the data shown on this graph.

   _____

   _____

   _____

   _____

Name _____ Date _____

29 Line Plot: Fish Stories

In a recent fishing derby, contestants caught a whole kettleful of fish. Look at the line plot below to see the weights of the fish that were caught. Then answer the questions.

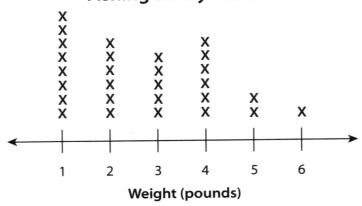

Fishing Derby Results

1. What was the most common weight of the fish caught at the derby?

   _____

2. How many of the fish caught weighed 3 pounds?

   _____

3. Which two weights appear with the same frequency?

   _____

4. What was the least common weight?

   _____

5. How many of the fish caught at the derby weighed more than 2 pounds?

   _____

Charts, Tables & Graphs

30 Line Plot: If the Shoe Fits . . .

At the end of the school year, the Lost-and-Found bin at the Hamilton
School was overflowing with sneakers and shoes. Tracy's malodorous job
was to record the sizes of the shoes and sneakers in the bin. Hold your
nose as you look at the line plot showing the results of Tracy's work. Then
answer the questions.

Lost-and-Found Footwear

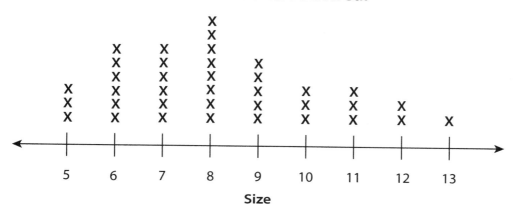

Size

1. What was the most common size of sneakers and shoes left in the bin?

    _____

2. How many sneakers and shoes were larger than size 9?

    _____

3. What was the least common size of footwear in the bin?

    _____

4. How many sneakers and shoes were smaller than size 7?

    _____

5. Based on this line plot, write a statement you can make about students' shoe sizes
    at Hamilton School.

    _____

31 Time Line: Olympic Sights and Sites

Didn't you just love watching the Olympics when they were held in Lake Placid, New York? But wait a minute, when was that? (Was I even born yet?) Check out the time line of Olympic events since 1960. Then answer the questions.

Sites of Olympic Games: 1960–2010

Summer Games			Winter Games
Rome, Italy	1960	1960	Squaw Valley, U.S.
Tokyo, Japan	1964	1964	Innsbruck, Austria
Mexico City, Mexico	1968	1968	Grenoble, France
Munich, West Germany	1972	1972	Sapporo, Japan
Montreal, Canada	1976	1976	Innsbruck, Austria
Moscow, USSR	1980	1980	Lake Placid, U.S.
Los Angeles, U.S.	1984	1984	Sarajevo, Yugoslavia
Seoul, South Korea	1988	1988	Calgary, Canada
Barcelona, Spain	1992	1992	Albertville, France
		1994	Lillehammer, Norway
Atlanta, U.S.	1996		
		1998	Nagano, Japan
Sydney, Australia	2000		
		2002	Salt Lake City, U.S.
Athens, Greece	2004		
		2006	Turin, Italy
Beijing, China	2008		
		2010	Vancouver, Canada

Source: *World Almanac and Book of Facts*, 2004

Olympic Sights and Sites *(continued)*

1. Where did the Winter Games take place in 1972? In 1984?

_____   _____

2. Where did the Summer Games take place in 1988? In 2000?

_____   _____

3. In what years were the Olympic Games held in Japan?

_____

4. Including 1960, how many times have the Olympic Games been held in the United States? In France?

_____   _____

5. In what year were the Olympic Games held in Moscow, USSR?

_____

6. On this time line, what is the only city that held the Olympic Games twice, and in what years?

_____

7. In what year were the Olympic Games held in Norway?

_____

8. What do you notice about the dates of Olympic events before and after 1992?

_____

32 Time Line: When Was That Invented?

Everybody learns about really famous inventions, such as the lightbulb and the automobile, but what about the really important stuff–like Velcro® or the zipper? Do you know when those were invented? Look at the time line below to find out. Then answer the questions.

The World's Most Important Inventions

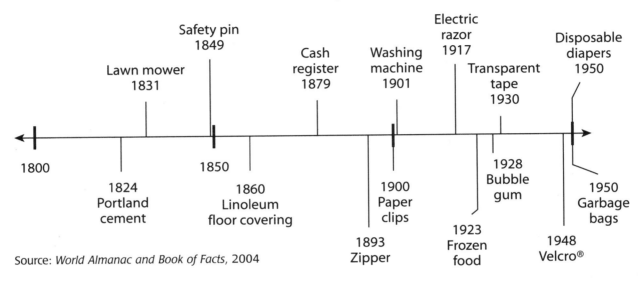

Source: *World Almanac and Book of Facts*, 2004

1. When was the safety pin invented? _____

2. When was frozen food invented? _____

3. What important item was invented in 1928? _____

4. Paper clips were invented in 1900. How long had linoleum floor covering been available before then? _____

5. Name two things invented in 1950. (Hmm, do you think these were coincidental?)

_____

_____

Charts, Tables & Graphs

Scholastic Teaching Resources

Name _____   Date _____

33 Stem-and-Leaf Diagram: Checkered Flags

Can you believe how fast those cars go in the Indianapolis 500, one of the world's most famous auto races? Look at the average speeds of the winning cars in this race since 1970. Then answer the questions.

Average Speeds (mph) of Indianapolis 500 Winners

Stem	Leaf
13	1 4 9
14	2 4 5 5 7 8 9
15	2 3 3 5 6 7 7 8 8 9
16	0 1 1 2 2 2 3 6 7 7
17	0 6
18	5

Source: *World Almanac and Book of Facts,* 2004

1. What was the highest average speed for a winner at Indianapolis?

   _____

2. What was the lowest average speed?

   _____

3. Among all of these winners, what was the most common average speed?

   _____

4. How many winners drove an average speed of 150 to 159?

   _____

5. How many winners averaged more than 160 miles per hour?

   _____

34 Stem-and-Leaf Diagrams: Hold on to Your Hats!

Mr. Carney owns an amusement park with several spine-tingling rides. Last summer he conducted a two-week study to see how many people rode each ride. Take a glimpse at the results shown in the stem-and-leaf diagrams below. Then answer the questions.

Octopus

Stem	Leaf
9	0 1 3
10	1 2 2 4
11	5 7 7 9
12	0 0 6

Scrambler

Stem	Leaf
7	0 0 0 2
8	0 4 5 5 6
9	3 7 8
10	2 5

Merry-Go-Round

Stem	Leaf
0	3 5
1	1 2 4 5
2	0 1 3
3	1 8
4	2 3 6

Roller Coaster

Stem	Leaf
15	0 1 3
16	4 4 8
17	6 7 7 9
18	3 5 5 6

Charts, Tables & Graphs

Scholastic Teaching Resources

Hold on to Your Hats! *(continued)*

1. What was the greatest number of people who rode the Octopus in one day?

   _____

2. Which ride had the fewest total riders?

   _____

3. What was the greatest number of people who rode the Scrambler in one day?

   _____

4. What was the most common number of riders per day on the Scrambler?

   _____

5. Which ride clearly had the most riders?

   _____

6. How many riders went on the merry-go-round on that ride's busiest day?

   _____

7. What was the smallest number of riders on the roller coaster in one day?

   _____

8. On how many days did more than 160 people ride the roller coaster?

   _____

9. On how many days did fewer than 100 people ride the Scrambler?

   _____

10. Which ride had the most days with 30 or fewer riders? _____

35 Scatterplots: Big Hair and Big Feet?

As you grow taller, does your hair get longer? As you get older, do your feet get bigger? Some curious researchers (who must be seriously underemployed!) studied 15 students to determine whether these factors are related. Look at the scatterplots below to see the results of their study. Then answer the questions.

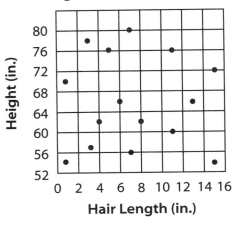

Height and Hair Length

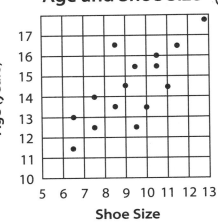

Age and Shoe Size

1. One of the students is 60 inches tall. How long is her hair? _____

2. How tall are the two students whose hair is 3 inches long? _____

3. One student is 14 years old. What is her shoe size? _____

4. Two of the students are 16 1/2 years old.
   What are their shoe sizes? _____

5. Do you see any trends in these scatterplots? Describe the data shown in each scatterplot and tell whether the data represent a trend.

   _____

   _____

   _____

   _____

Charts, Tables & Graphs

Name _____ Date _____

36 Scatterplots: Fast Food or Slow Food?

Does "fast food" make you smart? Does it help you run faster? These are interesting questions to think about as you munch on some chicken fingers and French fries. Professor Quisling conducted a survey of 20 students to see how many fast food meals they ate in a week, how they performed on a test, and how much they weighed. Look at the scatterplots below to see if these factors are related. Then answer the questions.

Fast Food and Test Scores   **Fast Food and Body Weight**

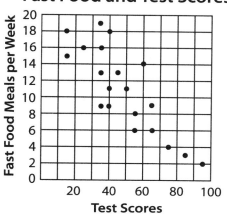
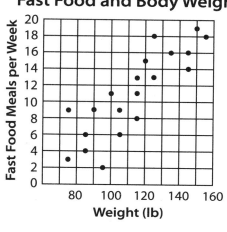

1. For the two students who got the highest test scores, how many fast-food meals did they eat in a week?
   _____

2. One student got a test score of 50. How many fast-food meals did the student eat?
   _____

3. How much does the heaviest student weigh, and how many fast-food meals did he or she eat?
   _____

4. How many students had more than ten fast-food meals during the week?
   _____

5. Describe the data shown on these scatterplots. Tell whether each plot shows a trend and, if so, what kind of trend.

   _____

   _____

   _____

   _____

Name _____ Date _____

37 Multiple Displays: Sweets and Treats

In some countries, people really like to eat candy. Some countries produce way too much garbage. And some countries do both! Check out these two graphs to learn about some "sweet" countries. Then answer the questions.

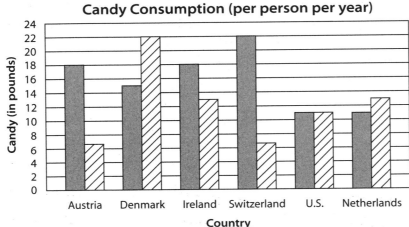

Candy Consumption (per person per year)

Source: *The Top 10 of Everything: 1998* (DK Publishing)

Garbage Production

Country	Pounds of Garbage Produced (per person per year)
France	🗑🗑🗑🗑🗑🗑
Germany	🗑🗑🗑🗑🗑🗑🗑🗑
Netherlands	🗑🗑🗑🗑🗑🗑🗑🗑🗑
Portugal	🗑🗑🗑🗑
Sweden	🗑🗑🗑🗑🗑
United States	🗑🗑🗑🗑🗑🗑🗑🗑🗑🗑🗑🗑🗑🗑🗑

Key: 🗑 = 100 lb   Source: *U.S. News and World Report* (June 28/July 5, 2004)

"Candy Consumption" is an example of a double bar graph. It gives two kinds of data for each country. Use the key to make sure you read it correctly.

When you see more than one display, it is very important to understand what each one presents. To answer questions, make sure you choose the correct display to find the information you need.

Charts, Tables & Graphs

Sweets and Treats *(continued)*

1. Which country consumes the most candy (both chocolate and other sweets) per person every year, and how much does each person consume?

   _____   _____

2. Which country produces the most garbage per person, and how much garbage does each person produce?

   _____   _____

3. In Austria, how many pounds of chocolate does the average person eat in a year?   _____

4. Which two countries seem to prefer chocolate to other kinds of sweets by a large margin?

   _____   _____

5. In France, how many pounds of garbage does the average person produce in a year?   _____

6. What do you notice about the kinds of candy consumed in the United States?

   _____

7. Which country produces the least garbage per person?   _____

8. If you wanted to calculate the total amount of garbage produced in Germany every year, what additional information would you need to know?

   _____

9. How many pounds of candy does the average person in Ireland eat every year?   _____

10. Which country consumes more "other sweets" than chocolate and—while they're eating—produces 1,100 pounds of garbage per person?

    _____

Charts, Tables & Graphs

Name _____   Date _____

38 Multiple Displays: People, People Everywhere!

Did you know that in the past 100 years, the world's population has tripled? We now live on the same planet as more than 6 billion other people. Mind-boggling, isn't it? Take a look at these displays to learn more about population growth. Then answer the questions.

World's Largest Cities: 1950 and 2000

1950		2000	
City	Population (in millions)	City	Population (in millions)
1. New York, U.S.	12.3	1. Tokyo, Japan	26.5
2. London, U.K.	8.7	2. São Paulo, Brazil	18.3
3. Tokyo, Japan	6.9	3. Mexico City, Mexico	18.3
4. Paris, France	5.4	4. New York, U.S.	16.8
5. Moscow, USSR	5.4	5. Bombay, India	16.5

Milestones in World Population Growth

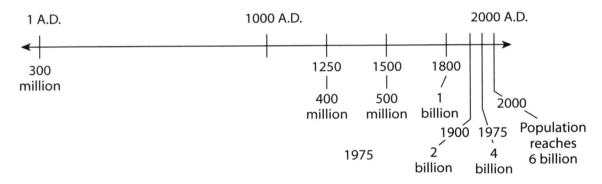

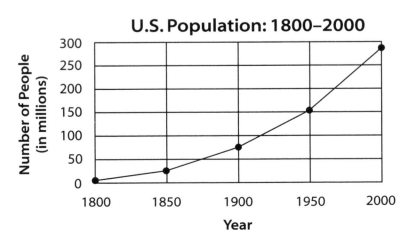

Source: *World Almanac and Book of Facts,* 2004

Scholastic Teaching Resources

Charts, Tables & Graphs

Name _____ Date _____

People, People Everywhere! *(continued)*

1. What was the world's population in 1250?   _____

2. When did the world's population first reach 1 billion?   _____

3. In 1950, what was the world's largest city (by population)?

   _____

4. How many of the world's top five largest cities in 1950 were still in the top five in 2000?
   Which cities?

   _____

5. What was the population of the United States in 1900?   _____

6. From 1950 to 2000, how much did the U.S. population grow?   _____

7. What was the world's most populous city in 2000, and how much had the city's
   population changed since 1950?

   _____

8. Based on the information in these displays, estimate the population of the United States
   in 2050.

   _____

9. In 2000, about how many people lived in Mexico City?   _____

10. What was the world's population in 1975?   _____

Answer Keys

1 Chart: That's a Long Time! (p. 6)
1. 67 days
2. Wim Hof (Netherlands)
3. 30 hours 59 minutes
4. 50 hours 55 minutes
5. Inge Wilda Svinjen (Norway)

2 Table: Cold Enough for Ya? (p. 7)
1. 1993 and 1999
2. Greatest number in 2003, fewest in 1993
3. In general, the event has become more popular each year. The number of participants increases each year.
4. The number of participants decreased (from 290 to 175). This change is probably related to the temperature, which dropped from 34°F to 10°F.

3 Circle Graph: And If You Believe THAT One . . . (p. 8)
1. Sudden illness
2. 23%
3. 20%, or $\frac{1}{5}$
4. Technical difficulties
5. Natural disaster

4 Pictograph: Better Skip the Dessert (p. 9)
1. Running
2. In-line skating
3. Jumping rope and step aerobics
4. About 9 1/2 hours
5. Bicycling

5 Bar Graph: The Need for Speed (p. 10)
1. Top Thrill Dragster
2. 120 miles per hour
3. Superman: The Escape and Tower of Terror
4. Dodonpa (Japan)
5. About 95 miles per hour

6 Line Graph: A Gassy Subject (p. 11)
1. About $0.29
2. The prices are almost the same; they changed very little in 10 years.
3. 1995–2005
4. The price has increased by almost $2.25 per gallon—nearly 10 times higher than the price in 1955.

7 Line Plot: Who Needs the Elevator? (p. 12)
1. 10.5 minutes
2. 15 racers
3. 13.5 minutes
4. 5 racers
5. In general, as the time increases, so does the number of racers.

8 Time Line: Oldies but Goodies (p. 13)
1. Lincoln Logs®
2. 1959
3. Slinky® and Legos®
4. 1952
5. Hula Hoop®

9 Stem-and-Leaf Diagram: Football Follies (p. 14)
1. 1 point
2. 64 points
3. 7 games
4. 8 games
5. 3 times

10 Scatterplot: Giant Pumpkins (p. 15)
1. About 1,330 pounds
2. 1998
3. 1999 and 2000
4. The data show that the giant pumpkins are generally getting heavier each year. This trend is positive because both values continue to increase.

Scholastic Teaching Resources

11 Constructing Graphs (pp. 16–17)
1. Answers will vary. Example:

Teens' Time

Chilling 25%
Playing sports 25%
Playing video games 15%
Watching TV 15%
Talking on phone 10%
Listening to music 10%

2. Answers will vary. Example:

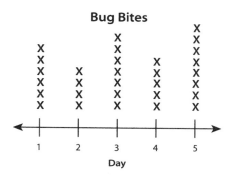

Bug Bites

3. Answers will vary. Example:

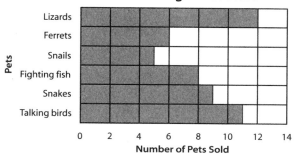

Sales at Margo's Pet Store

4. Answers will vary. Example:

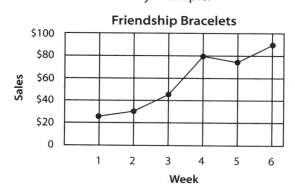

Friendship Bracelets

12 Representing Data (pp. 18–19)
1. a. Truman (42%) and Wilson (38%)
   b. The graph makes it look like Morse has one-half the votes, but he has only 15%. The fractions of the circle are not proportional to the percents.
2. a. It suggests that Dagen Has sells almost as much ice cream as Ted & Jimmy's. It is misleading because the vertical scale is not proportional; it jumps from 3 to 10 (thousands).
   b. It suggests that Ted & Jimmy's ice cream costs much more than Dagen Has, but only because the scale interval ($3.00 to $3.50) is misleading.
3. a. Both costs went up: $6.00 to $7.50 for tickets and $4.00 to about $5.50 for rentals.
   b. Because the graphs use different intervals (0, 6, 7, 8 and 0, 5, 10), it looks like movie ticket prices went up faster and higher than movie rental prices. But they both increased the same amount in the same period.

13 Charts: Hollywood Winners and Losers (p. 21)
1. *Titanic, Spider-Man,* and *Star Wars: Episode 1—The Phantom Menace*
2. *Star Wars* and *E.T.—The Extra-Terrestrial*
3. $600.8 million
4. *Star Wars*
5. $10 million
6. *Treasure Planet* and *The Adventure of Pluto Nash*
7. All 10
8. *Heaven's Gate*
9. $75 million
10. $10 million

14 Charts: Daredevils of Niagara Falls (p. 23)
1. Annie Taylor
2. Jean François Gravelet
3. 1876
4. Plastic barrel wrapped with rubber tubes
5. Both rode in a rubber ball with steel frame.
6. Peter Debernardi and Jeffrey Petkovich; Steven Trotter and Lori Martin
7. He crossed with a washing machine on his back.
8. 1985 and 1995
9. 6 minutes, 32.5 seconds
10. Andrew Jenkins

Answer Keys

15 Table: Wacky Weight Watchers (p. 25)
1. Jupiter
2. Pluto
3. 2.2 lbs on Venus; 2.8 lbs on Neptune
4. Jupiter
5. Saturn
6. Mercury and Mars
7. 210 lbs
8. 3,024 lbs on Mercury; 7,112 lbs on Uranus
9. Neptune
10. Answers will vary.

16 Tables: Feeling Sheepish (p. 27)
1. Australia
2. Falkland Islands
3. 5.81 sheep per person
4. 6
5. Falkland Islands and New Zealand
6. 48.1 million
7. The number of sheep (40.7 million) was less than half the human population (106 million).
8. 132.2 million
9. The sheep population has steadily decreased while the human population has steadily increased.
10. New Zealand, Uruguay, Australia, Mongolia, Kazakhstan, Somalia

17 Circle Graphs: A Pretty Penny (p. 29)
1. 1982–present
2. About $12\frac{1}{2}$ to 15 percent
3. 1837–1857, 1864–1962, 1962–1982
4. Less than 5%
5. Graphs will vary. Example:

Composition of a Penny

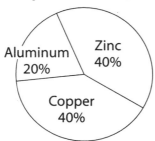

18 Circle Graphs: Sawing Wood (p. 31)
1. Adults
2. About 25%
3. More nightly snorers
4. About 30%
5. About 700 to 730
6. Graphs will vary. Example:

Percentage of People Who Snore

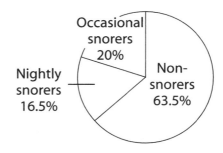

19 Pictograph: TV Nations (p. 32)
1. About 107 TVs per 1,000 people
2. Ethiopia
3. Algeria and Zambia
4. About 35 TVs per 1,000 people
5. Nigeria and Syria or Cameroon and Zimbabwe

20 Pictograph: Screaming for Ice Cream (p. 33)
1. About 32 pints
2. Canada
3. Belgium
4. United Kingdom and New Zealand
5. Denmark, Finland, and the United States

21 Pictograph: On Vacation—Wish You Were Here! (p. 34)
1. Germany and Spain
2. About 18 days
3. United States
4. 15 days
5. Australia, Britain, and the Netherlands

22 Bar Graph: Crazy Collections (p. 35)
1. Plastic bread-bag clips
2. About 1,400
3. Garden gnomes
4. About 800
5. About 3,300

Answer Keys

23 Bar Graph: That's a Whopper! (p. 37)
1. Bagel
2. Celery
3. All of them
4. Carrot
5. About 2,700 lbs
6. About 580 lbs
7. About 750 lbs
8. About 124 people
9. About 1,050 lbs
10. About 2,450 lbs

24 Bar Graphs: It's a Wonderful Life! (p. 39)
1. Hamster, squirrel
2. 5
3. 50 years
4. About 77 years old
5. 13 hours
6. About 28 years
7. Lemur
8. Koala
9. Human
10. About 24 years old

25 Line Graph: Colors to Dye For (p. 40)
1. 20
2. About 85
3. No, it does not indicate specific colors.
4. The number decreased (from 150 to 125).
5. About 100

26 Line Graph: Frog Heaven (p. 41)
1. About 210
2. It increased (from 210 to 380).
3. About 300
4. July and August
5. Probably zero

27 Line Graphs: Hello? Are You There? (p. 43)
1. About 5 million
2. 1997
3. About 35 million
4. About 120 million
5. 1999–2000
6. The number of users doubled each year.
7. 140 million
8. 250 to 260 million
9. 900 million to 1 billion
10. Both show rapid, steady growth.

28 Line Graph: Fore! (p. 45)
1. About $75,000
2. About $30,000
3. The women's leader earned ($231,000) less than half of what the men's leader earned ($531,000).
4. About $600,000 (from $231,000 to $863,000)
5. About $3.8 million
6. More than $1 million (from $75,000 to $1.2 million)
7. 2000
8. Answers will vary. Examples: Earnings for both men and women have increased steadily and rapidly since 1950. Earnings for women have been consistently and significantly lower than earnings for men.

29 Line Plot: Fish Stories (p. 46)
1. 1 lb
2. 5
3. 2 lbs and 4 lbs
4. 6 lbs
5. 14

30 Line Plot: If the Shoe Fits . . . (p. 47)
1. Size 8
2. 9
3. Size 13
4. 9
5. Answers will vary. Example: Most students wear sizes 6–9; only a few wear sizes larger than 9 or smaller than 6.

31 Time Line: Olympic Sights and Sites (p. 49)
1. Sapporo, Japan
   Sarajevo, Yugoslavia
2. Seoul, South Korea
   Sydney, Australia
3. 1964, 1972, 1998
4. 5 times in the U.S.; 2 times in France
5. 1980
6. Innsbruck, Austria, in 1964 and 1976
7. 1994
8. Through 1992, the Winter and Summer Games were held every four years in the same years; after 1992, the games alternated every two years.

32 Time Line: When Was That Invented? (p. 50)
1. 1849
2. 1923
3. Bubble gum
4. 40 years
5. Disposable diapers and garbage bags

33 Stem-and-Leaf Diagram: Checkered Flags (p. 51)
1. 185 mph
2. 131 mph
3. 162 mph
4. 10
5. 13

34 Stem-and-Leaf Diagrams: Hold on to Your Hats! (p. 53)
1. 126
2. Merry-go-round
3. 105
4. 70
5. Roller coaster
6. 46
7. 150
8. 11 days
9. 12 days
10. Merry-go-round

35 Scatterplots: Big Hair and Big Feet? (p. 54)
1. About 11 inches
2. 57 in. and 78 in.
3. $7\frac{1}{2}$
4. $8\frac{1}{2}$ and $11\frac{1}{2}$
5. There is no apparent trend in the first scatterplot; height and hair length are not related. Age and shoe size do seem to be related; the plot shows a positive trend.

36 Scatterplots: Fast-Food or Slow Food? (p. 55)
1. Two meals and three meals
2. 11 meals
3. About 155 lb; 18 meals
4. 11 students
5. The first plot shows a negative trend: as the number of fast-food meals increases, test scores decrease. The second plot shows a positive trend: as the number of fast-food meals increases, body weight increases, too.

37 Multiple Displays: Sweets and Treats (p. 57)
1. Denmark, 37 lbs
2. United States, about 1,630 lbs
3. 18 lbs
4. Austria and Switzerland
5. About 575 lb
6. The amounts of chocolate and "other sweets" are equal.
7. Portugal
8. The population of Germany
9. 31 lbs
10. The Netherlands

38 Multiple Displays: People, People Everywhere! (p. 59)
1. 400 million
2. 1800
3. New York City
4. Two; New York and Tokyo
5. About 75 million
6. It grew by 130 million from about 150 million to 280 million.
7. Tokyo; its population grew by almost 20 million.
8. 420 to 450 million
9. 18.3 million
10. 4 billion

Answer Keys